To Have; To Hold; To Heal

How I Survived

How I Forgave

How I Healed

Denise Peterson

Disclaimer

This memoir is a work of non-fiction based on the author's experiences, recollections, and interpretations. The opinions expressed in this memoir are solely those of the author and do not reflect the opinions or views of any affiliated organizations or individuals.

The author has not intended to malign, defame, or harm any person, entity, or group.

DEDICATION

This book is dedicated to every individual who feels like they're stuck in a situation.

THIS IS FOR YOU!!!!

This book is also dedicated to my three beautiful children; their tenacity and unwavering source of strength kept me going!

LOVE YOU ALWAYS!!!!

CONTENTS

FOREWORD

I pray as you read this book that, you will discover insight that will help you to become a better individual or even be able to encourage someone else to become a better version of themselves.

Also, as you read *To Have, To Hold, To Heal*, let me make it clear that this book was written in MY OPINION and my opinion only. I just wanted to paint a picture of where my mindset was at that time, right or wrong. Again, it was how I felt at that time in my life.

I'm thankful that this book came from a **BETTER** point of view and not a **BITTER** point of view, even though throughout different chapters, you will see some bitterness on display. It will show that, yes, we do get bitter about things that have or have not happened in our lives, but the best thing is we don't stay bitter; we use these situations to become better.

CHAPTER 1

WHO ARE YOU?

Are you really you? When you look into the mirror, who do you see? A mirror usually symbolizes self-reflection, truth, and clarity. Mirrors often encourage a deeper examination of one's identity and the truths that may be hidden within. When you're presented with the question, "Who are you?" someone is inquiring about the identity or nature of a person. They are seeking to understand more about the characteristics, maybe even the background of that individual.

It took me over 50 years to become who I am. WOW! Yes, over 50 years. Let me start out by telling you a little about me. I was born in New Haven, Connecticut. I had a beautiful upbringing with two loving and supportive parents. My parents did whatever they could to give my brother and me the world. You could say we were spoiled but not bratty. My parents weren't having that. I went to school through the New Haven school system. In my elementary days, I remember going to three different schools. Really don't remember why I had to change schools. We didn't move; we lived in the same house pretty much all of my upbringing. Oh yeah, I do remember; one of the schools had changed jurisdiction and the other had closed down. Then, in my eighth-grade year, I ended up going to a private catholic school.

Sidenote: That's something I never understood; why did "Christian" parents send their children to "catholic" schools? I don't believe it was because of religion. I personally think it was because catholic schools, at that time, were often perceived to offer a higher standard of education. They were known for having structured environments and strict discipline. The only thing I liked about going to a catholic school was because we wore uniforms. In my Christian background at this time, we weren't allowed to wear pants. So, I would roll up my pants, don't remember how I got them, and wear them under my skirt uniform, and when I got to school, I would roll them down. Later that day, before I got on the bus to return home, I would roll them back up or either take them off and put them in my bookbag. I know, things we do as kids.

By the time I was in Hillhouse High School, I was a straight-A student. I was in every club and because of my family entity, I was able to do whatever I wanted in the school. You couldn't tell me anything. But I was still yet humble and excited that I had reached a time and place in my life where I was happy with myself. Also, I was at a place where school was an outing besides church. Because at this time in my life, I was an advent churchgoer, and I LOVED it. I would look forward to those three to seven-day revivals. Watching people get healed and delivered while others were giving their lives to Christ. I was and still am the person you didn't want to look at when something funny happened during these revivals. Seeing wigs come off, slips falling down, but the most important thing was even though these funny actions had happened, these individuals were delivered and set free. Yes, the good old days.

Then, right in the middle of the second semester in my 10th grade, my parents decided to pick up and move to Camden, NJ, because of their servitude. I was fit to be tied. I was livid. What an impact that had on a sixteen-year-old who went from knowing just about everyone, most popular, to knowing nobody but family. I later thought about this - What we do as individuals, intentional or unintentional, will have an impact on those around us. Our words and behaviors can influence the emotions of others causing either happiness, sadness, anger, or even other feelings.

As we're traveling down the road to our new home, with only $32, my dad was a *faith* phenomenon; that's another book, I couldn't get myself together. The closer we got to New Jersey, the angrier I got. Yeah, I did like my new home, but it wasn't Connecticut. I believe I was moving in a shock mentality. Even though I believed in my parents' decisions, whether I agreed or not, I still had to go. I was supportive and confused all at the same time. Then it hit! Depression began to form. All I kept thinking was, why did this have to happen to me at this time in my life? My brother got acclimated pretty quickly. At first, he was like, oh my gosh, it was a bit of a shock especially coming from an uppity private school to a very challenging public school. He changed his name to a more masculine way of pronouncing it; too funny. To this day, he's still running with it. He made new friends and went on about his life. On the other hand, *I* became deeper and deeper into depression. My mom knew I loved shopping, but I just didn't have any desire at all to leave my lavender and purple bedroom. Don't judge me; it was sharp. My dad knew I loved to go to church, so he asked me if I wanted to go with him to Philadelphia to hear my uncle speak. I decided to go because I didn't say no to my father much at all. He didn't force me, he just simply believed he knew what might help me out of that frame of mind. Little did he know that it ended up helping me after all.

Let me tell you what happened; some of you might not believe it, but *it really did happen.* In between home and our destination was nothing but astounding. As my father was driving, I had gotten to the point that I just didn't want to be here anymore. I said to myself I had enough and just wanted to end my life. Here's what happened! As my father was driving to the destination, he had to go on a bridge to get across to Philadelphia. I looked back and noticed that an eighteen-wheeler truck was quickly approaching. I unlocked my door; there were no automatic door locks in this car. I looked at my father as if I was saying bye and began to open the door so I could fall out. To my amazement, the door got stuck. I turned around to see if the lock was still unlocked, and yes, it was, but the door would not open. I sat there in amazement. My father saw my face and I remember him asking me, are you okay and I quietly said yes. He kept driving to the destination, and once we got there, that door had no problem opening. All I could say to myself was there is a God who will keep you even when you don't want to be kept. Right then and there, I came to the realization that God had other plans for me. My life was and still is a part of a divine plan, despite my own intentions or efforts. God guided me toward a different outcome. Ever since that day, I had NO desire to try to take my life.

Sidenote: I sincerely/wholeheartedly *do not* recommend that anyone try what I did. Your ending might not turn out like mine. You can't take what's not yours!

So, as life began to move forward, I was so elated that my parents took that move. At this time, I didn't want to go back to Connecticut. As you read earlier, this was a totally different story a few years before. But when I graduated from Woodrow Wilson High School, I immediately went to Lincoln Business Institute, a business school. They were popular at that time. Lincoln is one of the very few business schools that is still around. I received an administrative certificate. After graduating from business school, I worked at some big companies, Campbell Soup, RCA and Rutgers University. I loved what I did. Had my own car, and life was good. I began working diligently in the ministry that my parents started; this was the reason for moving to New Jersey. People were joining; we were excited that the ministry was growing rapidly. And then … met a young man that came to the church with his mother. They were there for a few years. I began to listen to that self-doubt talk. You're getting older; you want children, family, and friends all getting married and going about their lives. Then the eyes started wandering on both sides; mind you, I was already close to his mother at this time.

Sidenote: When you have low self-esteem and someone from the opposite sex starts to show you some kind of attention, you tend to fall for them with blinders. Maybe not everybody and not all the time, but I did at this time. Where did that low self-esteem come from? I believe that I never fully bounced back from the initial move. I just got acclimated and went on about my life. Plus, I was really slender. People thought I had an eating disorder. It was just the total opposite. I loved to eat and still do, hahaha. So, I truly believe being ashamed of my body added to my low self-esteem. Being picked on in school didn't help either.

Let's fast forward…after five years of courting, that's what they used to call it, but today it's called dating or hooking up; I don't know, I can't keep up. But you would think you know someone. I really thought I did. But in reality, people let you see what they want you to see. You can't see what's in their hearts; you can't see what's on their minds. Sometimes, their actions will line up with what you want. Even though you still have an inclination, again, the blinders were on. At this time in my life, I started playing mind games with myself. You may ask, how is that? I started seeing some realities but did not see them. There are times when we don't want to see what is actually going on around us, so we begin to get in a place of denial.

So, I started asking myself who are you? I would ask myself this question often. I was fighting to find myself. I was and still am a daughter, a sister; was a wife; I eventually became the mother of three beautiful children, and much more. But I asked myself a question: will the real Denise stand up? I finally made up my mind that I was tired of being a prisoner of myself and took the courage to stand up.

After 28 years of marriage, I found out I wasn't who I wanted to be. Should I blame the individual, or should I just blame myself? You do realize that we allow people to treat us like they do, but is it really their fault? Then on the other hand, I also feel that if an individual is nurtured right, the true identity of the spouse would have eventually surfaced on both sides.

Let's go down memory lane! I got married one way - and divorced another way. You may ask, what exactly do you mean by that? In my experience (you'll hear that a lot in this book), I didn't feel like my true self on that wedding day. I had complex feelings. Even though a few months earlier I was asked, was this what I really wanted to do? Was I in love, or was it infatuation? NOOOO, I was a 25-year-old caught up in the facade of being a bride, having a big, beautiful wedding. Having 13 bridesmaids, each bridesmaid gown was designed by me, over 15 groomsmen, and limousines for the whole bridal party. My gown was a gown that I saw in all the well-known magazines, such as "The Elegant Bride" and "Modern Bridal." I had it flown in from New York along with my beautiful veil. The church was decorated beautifully. It was my fairy tale wedding coming true. We had over 250 guests. Both sides of my family had attended. It was the last time both of my grandmothers were together. Family and friends came from everywhere. Even through all that, I thought I was filling a void. Again, I wasn't who I wanted to be. Yes, I was happy, excited, and nervous all at once, who wasn't on their wedding day. But who was I? I was who I "thought" I was supposed to be at that time. I was a quiet and reserved young lady who always kept her eyes open to what was going on around her. Not paying attention to what was happening inwardly. I didn't focus on my inner feelings, my thoughts, or my emotional state. I got preoccupied with other things and wasn't mindful of my inner experiences. I was one who kept her thoughts and feelings private, but one thing I did do was have a journal or diary at that time. I truly believe writing my feelings and thoughts kept me on a path of integrity.

Let's get back to the wedding. I was on my way to becoming what we thought at the time was a "submissive" wife. Let's take a look at the meaning of submissive……ready to conform, that's *me*; meekly obedient, that's definitely ME. Wait, does that mean that you, as a woman (wife), are supposed to lose who you really are in submissiveness? No, not at all! I believe each partner should feel valued, respected, and free to express themselves. Losing one's sense of self leads to dissatisfaction and an imbalance in the relationship. I truly believe that both parties should support each other's growth and individuality while fostering a relationship based on mutual respect and equality.

As the years went by, the real Denise was begging to come forth. Little by little, who I wanted to be as a woman was coming to fruition, and the "submissiveness," as we thought it was, was quickly diminishing. Don't get me wrong, I feel it's easy to be submissive to someone who truly loves you, respects you, makes decisions with you, and is not just one-sided most of the time, someone who cares for your feelings and emotions because, in my opinion, you become submissive to each other, not taking away from the position of the man who is the head of the household. Some may agree or disagree, but again, this is *my* opinion and *my* experience. But for real, back in the day, I always personally thought the woman being "submissive" was more of the man "controlling" the marriage and not a togetherness. When I say "controlling," I'm referring to where "the man" will use excessive authority over various aspects of the relationship, limiting the choices or freedoms of their spouse. Also, where at times, "the man" made consistent choices, diminishing the input and wishes of their spouse. I wanted so badly to feel needed and wanted. As I was thinking, I wondered where and/or how this definition of controlling originated in my life. Especially, as growing up, I saw the total opposite. My parents were loving individuals who were married for over 35 years until my dad left this earth. Wait! Then I thought about it. My dad was nine years older than my mom. He ran our household very well. I remember him taking control but not in an excessive authority way. My mom humbly did what she had to do as a wife. Now, there were times she would speak her mind, and all you would hear my dad say was Shirl. They were funny together. As I mentioned, my parents were always supportive. My dad attended every sports game my brother played. He was my brother's best friend, and I was a daddy's girl. My dad was the most humblest and sweetest man I knew. He would do anything for anybody. Well, unlike my father portrayed, I believe control can be taken advantage of, especially when it's taken to a different level that's not appreciated by those around them.

Let's look at some examples of what I believe has an impact on a marriage. How about selflessness? It should be both ways, right? How about respect for your spouse? It should be both ways, right? The main two, how about trust and love, should be both ways, right? My point exactly! I know some may disagree because of what is stated in the bible in regard to a wife submitting, which I wholeheartedly believe. Personally, I believe a healthy relationship should thrive on balance, mutual respect, shared decision-making, and/or whatever is best for the individuals involved.

Because of what I thought submissiveness was, I lost myself as a woman. I came to find out that I wasn't honest with myself or my spouse. But answer me this,

How can you be honest when you already think you're living honestly?

At that time, I really thought I was living like I was "supposed" to live, not realizing I was actually damaging my self-esteem. I acted like everyone wanted and expected me to act, especially being a PK/preacher's kid, not just a preacher's kid, but a pastor's kid. A PK, which in itself was a battle at times. The reason I say battle is because again, living your life in plain view, do I do this; should I say that; should I go there while trying to uphold a parental standard was challenging. Things you did or said as a PK had a reflection on my parents and the church. There were times when I, as a young person, didn't always agree with some of the standards, but out of respect, you best believe you didn't say one word; you just went about your life and kept it moving. Again, who was I? I was a young lady who wanted to be loved and wanted to be free mentally and physically. When I say physically, I wasn't speaking about divorce at this time. Don't get me wrong, there were people and places that I was around that I literally was able to be Denise, but home wasn't one at times. Sure, there were times I actually really, truly believe I was happy. Being the "typical" wife, working, coming home cooking, and doing my wifely duties. I had three beautiful children at the times when I thought I was happy. I'll be happy one day. The next day, I would just tolerate things. Back and forth, back and forth! This went on for a while. But as time went on, I began to feel like I had chains on me. Not being able to relax my mind. I felt like I was on a mental roller coaster. I remember being nervous and shaky all the time. If I went out during the day to run errands, I would constantly be looking at my watch to make sure I was home in time. Now that I think about it, I was feeling like this a year after I got married, thinking it was the norm.

After five years of marriage, we decided to start a family. I was excited and couldn't wait to start a family. Another void is being filled. Having my three children was the best thing that happened to me. To be a good mother while dealing with unexpected life situations was one of the hardest roles I've ever had to play.

There were times I actually felt like a married, single mother. But I wonder why when all, I say all, the household bills were paid, even though I didn't know what they were. I did not have to worry about one household bill, but I still felt like I was in a world of my own. Was I not grateful? Very much so, but when you're feeling like you're in a box and can't get out and not being heard, some things that were being done in a positive realm became unnoticed.

I then began to notice the distrust —- Hear me out! What happens when you trust someone enough to pour out your heart and your feelings, and they use what you told them against you to enhance their very own actions? Unbelievable! The downward spiraling had begun.

The emotional, psychological, and financial aspects progressively became worse.

With everything that was happening, I allowed bitterness, regrets, and resentment to set in. Why is it so important to let go of regrets (disappointments)? Letting go of regrets is crucial because dwelling on past hurts and past mistakes can hinder personal growth and happiness. You may ask how. Here are a few ideas I feel will assist us better in our daily lives:

1. When you're constantly focusing on past hurts and past errors, it often means you aren't focusing on the lessons that could teach you.
2. Constantly focusing on past hurts and mistakes can lead to feelings of guilt, shame, and regrets.
3. Holding on to regrets can stall your personal development because your fixed mindset can prevent you from embracing challenges and opportunities for improvement.
4. When you're so preoccupied with the past, you tend to miss out on current opportunities.
5. Regrets, if not dealt with, can lead to lingering resentment.

To have personal growth and happiness, it's essential to acknowledge and learn from past mistakes without letting them dominate your thoughts.

I read somewhere that you should never trust your tongue when your heart is bitter. Bitterness can and will distort your judgment and your thinking, making it very hard to communicate honestly. In my case, I really didn't speak much but I couldn't trust my thoughts. I was experiencing confusion and self-doubt. Yet, I was working in ministry every week and was good at it (if I must say so myself). No one knew the inward battle that I was dealingwith because I knew how to hide it.

I came across this powerful message that deeply resonated with me. This message read:

✳

You couldn't heal because you kept pretending you weren't hurt.

✳

The more I pretended or hid, the longer it took to heal.

CHAPTER 2

WHAT'S ON YOUR MIND

The mind is a complex of mental abilities that enables consciousness, perception, thinking, judgment, and memory. It includes a range of mental activities, including reasoning, emotions, imagination, and decision-making. I read that the mind is responsible for processing information, forming thoughts, and guiding behavior.

As I was studying the mind, I came across the definition of the mindset and mind frame. So many individuals often believe they mean the same. Actually they are related in concepts but are not the same. Let me explain! The mindset refers to a person's established set of beliefs that may influence how they feel and behave. A mind frame usually refers to the temporary state of one's thoughts and feelings at a particular moment. I believe that the mind frame is more about the immediate mental and emotional context in which an individual is operating. In short form, a mindset is an individual being more stable and long-term, while a mind frame is temporary or short-lived. Yup, they're right; a mind is a terrible thing to waste.

Some of us were brought up in an era where getting divorced was not as prevalent as it is today. I genuinely felt the same way. I heard chattering around me, saying to love the "hell" out of them. I actually thought I was doing that, but then I asked myself,

How can you love somebody so strongly when you don't even know how to love yourself?

I then became bound internally and emotionally because the challenges I was facing led to deep-seated fears, anxieties, and unresolved emotions. My thoughts, feelings, and behavior became negatively affected. That healthy bond was being diminished. Then I asked myself was the bond ever there? Maybe not, especially when one side was feeling that they couldn't trust one another or communicate openly. I feel that a lot of the time when speaking with people, we listen to speak and not listen with open ears. We become self-focus. Sometimes, individuals prioritize their own thoughts and opinions, which can make them more focused on what they want to say rather than truly understanding who's speaking. A lot of times, individuals feel more comfortable when they can steer the conversation, more like being in control. In my perspective, a listening ear involves fully understanding, fully responding, and remembering what the individual is saying. Little do we realize that this approach brings about a better way to communicate, a deeper understanding, and it brings about stronger relationships.

I was believing in something outwardly, but feeling something differently inwardly. What this statement means is that I would show support in something, but privately or internally have doubts or different feelings. Not realizing that this reflects a conflict between one's public actions and their private thoughts or emotions. Believe it or not, this happens more than we know. I personally did this because I didn't want to "be the one" to cause division or cause some type of confusion. So, I continued to keep quiet. At times, it wasn't the best decision to make. I started to see that in my later years. I started going along with things just to avoid conflict or confrontation despite my true feelings. Why hide my true feelings? Maybe because I wanted to protect myself from being vulnerable and being judged. It became a mental battle within myself, but yet, Denise was there to uplift and encourage everyone else while fighting through her own mental state. Boy, I found out that you can't put everyone first forever. Don't get me wrong, it's definitely ok to help and care for others, it makes you feel good when you help others, but not when you're constantly neglecting your own needs. Sometimes, this can lead to resentment. That's not in all relationships because we, as parents, will always be there for our children (the majority of us). So many times, we live our lives wanting so badly to please others, regardless of how it makes us feel. We allow other people to design our lives by allowing them to control our decisions, our actions, and overall our life directions. This is not always bad, depending on the person and/or the situation, especially when you're both in agreement with the outcomes and the outcomes are for your betterment. I so desperately wanted that person or persons to see my full potential and push me to be a better individual. Then, later, realizing they couldn't see the full potential in me because they themselves weren't living their own full potential.

That mental battle was carried out for so many years that it became who I was. Why? Because the internal struggles and challenges began to shape my inward characteristics. We do realize our character becomes our destiny, and it also influences the decisions we make. It began to define how I thought and how I felt at times in various situations.

We waste so much time because of the stories we tell ourselves that we do even have the nerve to start believing them. We often suffer more in imagination than in reality because our minds have a tendency to magnify potential negative outcomes. When I say magnifying potential outcomes, I'm referring to imagining the worst possible scenario and believing it's more likely to happen than it actually is. For example, you might make a small mistake at work, and here you go, starting to magnify the negativity by thinking, oh well, I made this mistake, and now I'm going to be fired. Boo, it's not even all that. Here's another example! You may see a family member or friend upset - your negativity magnification immediately starts believing it's because of something you did. It can be totally unrelated. If you're not careful, this type of thinking will bring on unnecessary anxiety and stress. Later in this chapter, you will read suggestions that can combat this way of thinking.

Ok, back to me… I was determined not to let my mental state define who I wanted to become in the future. One day, I looked in the mirror and said to myself will the real Denise please stand up? From there on, let me tell you, my whole life has completely transformed for the better. My mind, body, and soul were beginning to flourish like a butterfly coming out of its cocoon. People at that time didn't understand what was going on with me. I was so tired of allowing other people's opinions to become mine, not really agreeing, and not having a voice of my own.

I needed to be a voice and not an echo.

Not realizing that my voice was worthy of being heard. We must realize that no one else has our experiences, thoughts, or feelings. Remember, you are unique! Keep in mind that when you speak, you empower others who might have the same views but are too hesitant to speak up. I've been there and done that plenty of times.

When I came out of my mental prison (I do go back to visit every now and then, but I don't stay there), it was the best feeling ever. I felt like chains were finally broken; I was beginning to feel a sense of freedom. I felt like I was in a new world, and nothing wasn't going to stop me. Then I went right back to what I "thought" was my reality and went right back to that negative mental state of mind for another 14 years; yes, I said 14 years. You may ask why! Again, at that time, being so mentally confused, I was STILL living in the voice of what *"I"* thought others were saying or what *"I"* thought people were thinking. Trying to please everyone else but myself.

Let me make one thing clear. When I say I was mentally confused, I wasn't so crazy that I needed to be in a mental institution NOOO (that's funny). It was my lack of confidence that prevented me from being my authentic self. Why so much lack of confidence? Fear of judgment! Worrying about what others thought. This way of thinking allowed me to suppress my true thoughts, feelings, and behavior just to avoid criticism or rejection. Lack of confidence sometimes resulted in seeking approval from others instead of expressing my own personality. Also, having a lack of confidence assisted in avoiding taking risks and/or trying new opportunities. When we don't take risks, it sometimes can lead to being stuck in your comfort zone. Another reason for a lack of confidence can be self-doubt. Doubting your abilities and worth, second guessing your choices, and hesitating to stand by your very own choices. Then, you begin to rely on other individuals to define your actions and beliefs. Building confidence can take some time because you have to consistently talk positively to yourself and gradually step out of your comfort zone.

I remember feeling like I was never heard, feeling like my voice didn't count. It felt like I was living day by day, moment by moment. It felt like my words were rejected. I remember feeling like nobody wanted to hear what I had to say. Even when I spoke, it was like, 'Oh ok,' and that's it. I allowed so much to live rent free in my mind, so much negativity, and the thoughts of others, how they may or may not perceive me. Sometimes, we as individuals deposit our insecurities on others, especially our children, and most of the time, the insecurities become who we are. Why do insecurities become a part of our identity? Believe it or not, they shape our thoughts, our behaviors, and our perceptions, and over time, the negative self begins to become deeply ingrained. Insecurities can come about because of past experiences. Sometimes, what we tell ourselves can come from negative feedback. I heard from so many that they were told when they were young, either by a parent or some other individual that they wouldn't amount to anything. They would never be anything. This type of communication can definitely bring on insecurities. I was blessed to have never been told that. The insecurity that I had strictly came from my own thoughts of uncertainty.

It can take years for those insecurities to be dropped, and then they still have a hold on us depending on where our mindset is. Again, my confidence level was pretty low, especially whenever I was alone. I came to notice that when you don't pursue confidence, people tend to treat you like you're less than others, overlooked, and/or passed over for opportunities. Sometimes taken advantage of and/or ignored, like your opinion and ideas may be dismissed or ignored, again, MY opinion and MY experience. Or perhaps not less than, but feel they will treat you like you're a timid or shy individual. Some may say I was an introvert. What's an introvert, you asked? One definition is… a person who tends to be more focused on their inner thoughts and feelings rather than seeking external stimulation. As I got older, I began to start paying a lot more attention to my inner feelings by just sitting quietly and observing what was around me. Also, by spending time alone without distractions. Listening to uplifting music that fed my mind and soul allows me to reconnect with myself and process thoughts and emotions to help me find clarity and peace.

From my perspective, being an introvert, I believe some individuals REALLY don't know how to interact with introverts. I believe some individuals don't understand because, in my experience, people don't know what to say or do around those individuals who are introverts. You will either be intimidated because you're not sure of what they're thinking, there are some who will just wait to see how we react to certain situations, or they will try to "control" you. Not knowing that you know what's happening the whole time (I have to smile on that one). Being an introvert doesn't mean you're dumb or can't comprehend what's going on around you. I came to realize that sometimes it's good to "play" dumb to see how people move. Being a quiet person is not always a bad thing. Some quiet individuals often enjoy their own company and are comfortable with solitude, which can lead to greater self-reliance and independence. Sometimes, their calm demeanor can be reassuring to others and help to de-escalate tense situations. Overall, being quiet can contribute to a person's strength and resilience in various aspects of life. You learn to sit back and watch. You can learn a lot by watching.

I once read that our thoughts (the mind) play a pivotal part in who we are and who we will become. The reason is that our thoughts determine how we interpret and respond to different elements. Think about it: if you think about a past failure, it might make you feel sad or anxious, which could impact your current actions. You'll find yourself upset with someone who is currently around you, and they have no idea why you're upset with them. Our thoughts influence how we perceive the world around us. Take notice; if you're in a positive frame of mind, you are more likely to notice positive details in your environment and vice-versa with negativity. We realize that negative thinking can result in stress, while positivity can lead to resilience and a proactive attitude. We all heard the saying, what we think about, we bring about. That's why it is so important to feed our minds positively on a daily basis. These are a few reasons why building your mental capacity in a positive way is so important:

1. It builds positive thoughts; it helps reduce stress and anxiety.

2. Building your mental capacity helps with your self-confidence, helping you to believe in your abilities and your worth.

3. One of my favorites is that I believe it builds resilience (the ability to recover quicker than usual from difficulties or significant sources of stress), enabling you to better cope with challenges and setbacks.

What I love most is that as we incorporate positive activity into our lives, it will eventually lead to personal growth and a balanced life, and it will become who we are. Remember, a powerful mind can achieve anything it desires. Yes! Mental strength, determination, and focus are key factors in achieving goals. The power of the mindset helps us to bounce back through troubled times and overcome the obstacles that life throws at us. It also helps reduce the stress levels we may experience during difficult times, making it easier for us to cope and recover.

One of the reasons why I'm writing this book is to encourage everyone, no matter your religion, your race, or your age, to be true to yourself! To be more confident in who YOU are. To believe in your own abilities. For me and so many others, this type of confidence doesn't happen overnight. It took me some time, and I'm still working on it. What helped me to be more confident was prayer and therapy. Yes, therapy (I'm not opening that bag right now). Some individuals don't believe in therapy, your choice.

Well, I believe that prayer was my weapon, and therapy was my strategy. What I'm saying is we all have those voices that come to distract us and try to manipulate us and I feel when you're not as confident, you tend to listen more to the negative side. I used to tell my children, no matter where you go or who you're around, to always be you. Because people talk when you do bad, they talk when you do something good. People will always have some type of opinion, so why not be YOU?

Remember, their opinions don't define your reality.

Let me tell you a factual story of one person's opinion, my grandmother. Back in the early 90's, I was in my early 20s, and I had to speak at a church event. This event was held at a school gymnasium. It was not a school event; the church was just using the gymnasium. I will never forget it, let me tell you why. At the end of event, they had asked my grandmother if she wanted to have something to say since she was visiting us from Connecticut. She got up and began to elaborate on how proud she was of me and I'm sitting there smiling UNTIL she began to speak 'her opinion'. She spoke in her authoritative voice and yelled that she thanked God that her granddaughter was a virgin. Yes, in front of all those people and those who came with me. Her opinion! She didn't know if it was true or not. All I could do was put my head down and say I hope I never see these people again. She spoke HER opinion. She didn't know if it was my reality or not. Today, I can sit back and laugh. Rest in peace, grandma! But can you even imagine where my mindset might have been? To this day, I never knew why she felt the need to even say that. It literally took me a couple of days to get my mindset back to a, I want to say, a 'normal' way of thinking.

I came to the realization that your mindset is everything. It shapes our perceptions, it also influences our reactions. If we allow it, it can hinder our progress and fulfillment in life. It also shapes your world and your reality. We have all heard this saying: a negative mindset will never give you a positive life.

Take back your God-given power through your mind, listen to your heart, and replace negative self-talk with positive affirmations. We have to consistently affirm our worth. Consistently affirming your worth helps build and maintain self-esteem, counteracts negative self-talk, and reinforces a positive self-image. The one thing I truly love about being consistent in affirming your worth is it helps to "internalize" positive beliefs. How? By regularly reminding yourself of your strengths, your accomplishments and your positive qualities. Also, avoiding toxic environments that reinforce those negative beliefs, such as being around individuals who constantly criticize, belittle, or manipulate, can erode self-esteem and reinforce negative thinking. Even some high-stress work environments with your management, lack of support, and toxic colleagues can contribute to a negative mindset.

Sidenote: By writing this statement, am I suggesting that you leave your employment if it's toxic? NO! That's just an example of a toxic work environment. Another way is to start treating yourself with the same kindness and understanding that you offer to someone else. Recognize your own worth. When you consistently affirm your worth, those positive beliefs will become a natural part of yourself. There are people, places, and things that are ready to diminish our worth if we allow it. We have given our power to others through our minds. Let me explain. We allow other people's opinions, expectations, and judgments to dictate our decisions and self-worth. Then, we began to start internalizing criticism, which eventually diminished our confidence. Then worrying starts to manifest. Worrying if I said something wrong or If I didn't do the right thing. Chronic worrying can reinforce negative thought patterns, making it harder to see positive aspects of life. A lot of times, we don't realize that.

Excessive worry can sometimes manifest the very thing we're worrying about.

When you think about it, internalizing criticism and worrying both involve focusing on negative aspects. They both create a cycle of repetitive and unproductive thinking, where the individuals constantly replay the criticism or worry without finding a resolution.

Even as I was writing this book, I started thinking about what would this one say about certain things, what would that one say? I had to stop and bring my thoughts back to the fact that this book is MY opinion, and if people can't accept that, oh well. If they see me in a different way after reading this book, oh well.

What others think of you is none of your business.

I also realized that we may feel broken at times because of what somebody said or did but I guarantee you that you WILL be whole again as long as YOU take the necessary steps to properly heal. It's important to acknowledge these feelings and seek support, whether through friends not associates - big difference, through trusted family, through professional help, or mainly through God to help navigate us through some tough times. In my case, I spoke to various individuals at times; some advice was good, and some not so good. But I had to decide what was best for me.

Why, as a society, do we care so much about what others think? Hmmm! I believe we care because of the desire for social acceptance and belonging. We, as humans, are primarily social creatures. Sometimes, our survival depends on being part of a group. We will prioritize what others think and will diminish our own thoughts. Been there, done that! But not anymore; thank God for mental maturity.

When you're not happy with who you are, you'll start finding fault in things around you. We do realize that when individuals aren't happy, they often project their dissatisfactions onto their surroundings as a way to cope. A lot of times, unhappiness is used to shift the focus away from oneself. The saying goes - 'Misery loves company,' and being miserable is not a comfortable place. Especially when there are people living together, and you're all miserable. Oh boy, here we go! Here comes the constant fault finding and the toxicity. No peace at all! This went on for a while, hoping things would get better. Sometimes, one would work towards making things better, and the other would be so mentally tired that they couldn't accept the good behaviors. Year after year, same old same old! Let me ask this…

How can you be peaceful mentally when your surroundings aren't peaceful?

I eventually, after some years, had to create a mental safe space where I was able to relax and recharge. But before that, I had to change my mindset by beginning to focus on the positive around me. I had to maintain calmness despite the chaos. I literally had to cultivate a positive outlook and practice gratitude to shift my focus from turmoil to internal contentment. This was a struggle at times, but it can be done.

I truly believe it when they say misery loves company. That's true for the majority of people, but for me, if I became upset about anything, I quickly became withdrawn and stayed to myself, what I call the bubble effect. What's the bubble effect, you asked? For me, it was when I got upset, and as I previously said, I would isolate myself. I wanted to be disconnected and detached from the world around me.

Here comes those thoughts. Let me tell you if you're not prayed up and/or continually speaking positivity to yourself daily, you will fall for that negative voice. As you read the last few chapters, you will then see what I personally did to become a better version of myself.

Learn to train your mind to be stronger than your feelings.

Let me tell you something: when you finally get to a point where you no longer will continue to live YOUR life in the voice of what somebody else said or did, it's a very liberating feeling. The best weight to lose is the opinion of others. We already know what opinions are like; everyone has them. Let's be honest: when someone speaks about something we might have either said or done, we begin to ponder on it. But the best thing is whether it is right or wrong, it's "their" opinion, and we have to remember to prioritize our own well-being over external validation.

There comes a time when you have to learn (It takes a lot of practice) to bulletproof your mindset. Bulletproofing your mindset involves developing mental toughness and resilience to handle challenges and setbacks effectively. Also, to avoid negative influences that drain your energy. Listen, if there's something that is beyond your control, do you realize that it's best to release it and let it go from your thoughts? Holding on to things beyond our control can lead to unnecessary stress and anxiety (among other things). It's often more beneficial to focus on what we can influence and accept than focus on the things that are out of our hands. Letting go can bring peace and allow us to direct our energy toward positive actions and decisions within our control.

Make yourself strong enough to survive alone.

CHAPTER 3

FORGIVE OR NOT TO

FORGIVE?

The dove carrying an olive branch conveys the message of forgiving past grievances and moving forward in peace.

Forgive me first! I had to forgive myself first for any mistakes, intentional or unintentional, that I contributed to the divorce without blaming myself entirely. I had to recognize that everyone makes mistakes. Making mistakes provides opportunities to learn and grow. It provides opportunities to make amends, which can be a very important step in the healing process. Denying any mistakes could prevent my healing. When mistakes aren't acknowledged, it hinders personal growth and hinders the opportunity for resolution. Also, realizing that I'm not alone in experiencing the hard emotions, I had to find ways to be thankful for how this experience has shaped me. Had to be patient with myself and continue letting myself know that my healing was about to take place. Being patient takes a process. I had to acknowledge my emotions. Acknowledging your emotions can be rough, but it's the first step in the forgiving process. I had to understand that feeling a range of emotions, such as grief, anger, confusion, and relief, was normal, and I also took time to reflect on what I was feeling. I had to allow myself to experience these emotions without judgment. This one was very challenging, but I had to try to stay in the present and not dwell excessively on the past. I also had to release any beliefs about how I "should" feel. Emotions are natural responses and don't always align with our expectations. What we forget is that having patience with yourself is a type of self-love and plays a big part in the healing process. Having patience with yourself will allow you to accept your flaws and bring about a compassionate view of yourself. It will help you to build resilience, make better decisions, and reduce self-criticism. Patience will also help you to stay calm, in various situations, reducing anxiety and stress. Additionally, patience enables you to stay committed to long-term goals without getting discouraged by short-term setbacks. Having patience with yourself will translate into having patience with others. Self-patience contributes to a more peaceful and content state of mind.

I remember beating myself up mentally for allowing myself to agree with people, places, and things that I either didn't want to be a part of but still went or said anyway. I often spoke what I thought others wanted to hear, but at the same time, saying to myself that's not what you wanted to say.

I had to forgive myself for not speaking my TRUE self.

Why couldn't I say what I was truly feeling? We do realize that expressing our true feelings can be challenging at times for different reasons due to the fact that we may have a fear of judgment, rejection, or negative responses from others. Sometimes, being open about feelings makes us feel vulnerable, exposing parts of ourselves that we might prefer to keep hidden. It may also have been because sometimes we have trouble understanding and speaking one's true emotions, especially when we lack confidence. Many people won't speak their truth because of fear of conflict. They try to avoid disagreements to prevent conflicts, even if it means not being true to their own beliefs. Later, regretting the fact that you didn't stand up for your own views. There are times we agree with others because, as I mentioned, the confidence just isn't there. I had to forgive myself for the negative survival patterns and traits I picked up while enduring. Some of these negative survival patterns and traits were resentment, bitterness, distrust, and low self-esteem. I had to take some steps to get rid of these patterns. Steps like challenging my negative thoughts by replacing them with positive and realistic ones. I also had to learn to assert my needs and rights without being aggressive; in other words, standing up for myself. Had to ensure my own boundaries and respect. I also had to educate myself by reading books on personal development and/or listening to certain motivational speakers. But most of all, I had to forgive myself for the past and keep moving forward.

I owe myself the biggest apology for putting up with what I didn't deserve.

Forgiveness - an "intentional" decision to release feelings of resentment and anger or the desire for revenge towards a person or people that you feel may have hurt you. Forgiving does not necessarily mean excusing the behavior NOPE, but it does mean making a "conscious" decision to release negative feelings and to not hold the wrong against the person(s). There are various levels to forgiveness; here's a few:

Decisional Forgiveness: Forgiveness that involves someone making a conscious decision to forgive but seeks a non-vengeful commitment.

Emotional Forgiveness: This forgiveness is a deeper level involving letting go of negative emotions like anger, resentment, or bitterness towards the person who caused you harm.

Conditional Forgiveness: This forgiveness is based on certain conditions, like an apology by the individual who hurt you.

Unconditional Forgiveness: Forgiveness that involves letting go of resentment, anger and the desire for retribution towards someone who has wronged you, without any conditions or expectations.

Self-Forgiveness: This is one I wrote about earlier in this chapter. Self-forgiveness involves forgiving oneself for past mistakes or wrongdoings. This form of forgiveness was, and still is, so important to me because of the mental and emotional health attached. It allowed me to move past the guilt or shame that may have tried to arise.

Sometimes, the individual(s) might not deserve your forgiveness, but do it for YOU. You do realize that the person who has the most power in your life is the person you have not forgiven. Forgiveness helps us to move forward and can be freeing for the persons offering it. Without forgiveness, our souls are tied to whatever happened. It's more about releasing the hold that the past has on you than condoning the behavior of those who hurt you. Plenty of times, we all heard the saying, "Forgive and forget."

This "forgive and forget" phase is one we often use to encourage people to move past conflicts and grievances. This phase does not literally mean erasing the memory of the wrongdoing from your mind. If you can, that'll be phenomenal. I believe it implies not dwelling on the past hurt and not allowing it to affect your present, your future interactions, or your decisions. What I love is that I feel it's about not letting the past control your emotions or actions. It's about maintaining an emotional balance and making decisions on your present circumstances and future goals rather than being influenced and/or hindered by past negative experiences. This chapter is about forgiveness, and practicing forgiveness letting go of grudges, and focusing on growth and positive outcomes instead of being driven by old hurts or mistakes that will help you to maintain an emotional balance.

Changing the story you tell yourself about the past will help you to contain your emotions and/or actions. This process involves recognizing and altering negative narratives or beliefs that may be holding you back, allowing you to view past events with a new perspective that fosters growth, resilience, and better emotional regulation. Instead of seeing yourself as a victim, even though you may be a victim, you'll consider how the experience has contributed to your growth. You'll also realize how the experience helps find positive outcomes in different situations.

But in my opinion, there are some things you just can't forget. The reason is that hurtful experiences can leave deep emotional scars, thus making it challenging to let go of the pain and anger associated with the event, especially if the hurtful experiences are repetitive.

Trust issues became relevant again, as in the earlier chapter. Once trust is broken, it can definitely be difficult to rebuild. Allow trust is to be rebuilt gradually based on consistent positive actions, not just words. People may forgive but will still remember to protect themselves from future harm, whether it's necessary or not. Forgiving someone doesn't mean you should leave yourself vulnerable to future harm. Some individuals especially don't want to forget because they may feel that forgetting means letting the wrongdoer off the hook, which seems to be unfair to some individuals. There have been times that I didn't want to forgive or forget. Was I wrong? A big yes! Until I came to the conclusion that unforgiveness wasn't helping me at all. It was causing me more pain, preventing me from moving forward, and keeping me stuck in negativity. We actually think that it's hurting the other individual(s), but in all essence, we're the ones being affected. Unforgiveness can and will damage your own mental state and your health. How? Harboring or holding on to unforgiveness can lead to chronic stress, anxiety, and depression, just to name a few. If not dealt with, these constant negative emotions can trigger the body's stress response, leading to physical symptoms like headaches, high blood pressure, and a weakened immune system.

The more resentment released from my thoughts, the more love I had to express.

Releasing those negative thoughts made room mentally for love and compassion to be expressed. It's like cleaning out the clutter and making room for something new and beautiful. It's also like putting a leaf in a stream of water and watching it float away. Ohhhh, the inner peace it brings! Ultimately, releasing resentment can also lead to a sense of inner peace and contentment. When an individual is not bogged down by negative emotions, you can experience a more profound sense of joy and fulfillment in your daily life. Releasing negative emotions creates a space for positive thoughts and actions to take over. Dave Willis, the writer, wrote that holding a grudge doesn't make you strong; it makes you bitter. He went on to say that forgiving doesn't make you weak; it sets you free. This Is a powerful statement because holding grudges will weigh you down, while forgiveness gives you inner strength and resilience and will allow you to face future challenges with greater fortitude.

I have seen, in my lifetime, how unforgiveness has damaged many families, not only because of unforgiveness but sometimes pride has set in. Nobody wants to be the one to "give in." If we're not careful, eventually, hate will set in. I saw how it created barriers between family members. I saw how individuals were expressing themselves in hurtful ways. It's disheartening to see how the unforgiving pattern was passed down from generation to generation, which made it more difficult for families to rely on one another and support one another.

Martin Luther King, Jr. said, "Let no man pull you low enough to hate them."

Wow! Now, that's a powerful statement. I love this statement because it lets us know not to allow others' negative actions or behaviors to cause us to feel hatred. Instead of responding to negativity with more negativity, the 'idea' is to rise above it and maintain one's own integrity and positivity. The word here is 'idea'. Speaking for myself, we don't always rise above negativity, especially when it's presented to you unexpectedly. Human nature wants to react the same way it was presented to you. But, we have to just close our mouths at times, think about what was said, and then respond. Let me say this: I'm definitely still working on myself in this synopsis.

When I first got divorced, I didn't want to forgive but desperately wanted to forget. I believe I didn't want to forgive because sometimes forgiveness brings us back to the details of our past. It involves revisiting and processing specific events, emotions, and experiences that caused the hurt or resentment in the first place. On the positive side of that, it also helps us to understand the motives and circumstances behind the actions of others and ourselves and will give new meaning to the situation. Also, by forgiving, I felt that it had put me in a place of vulnerability, fearing that forgiving could lead to being hurt again in the future. I didn't realize the toll that holding onto unforgiveness was taking on my mental well-being and my health. I was still bound "thinking" I was free. When we don't forgive, all those negative incidents that we want to forget will still weigh heavy on us. Why? Because the emotional wounds remain open. In my case, I still found myself thinking about the past in a negative way, even though everything wasn't negative all the time.

After the divorce, those negative thoughts were the only thing occupying my thoughts. Why? Because I wasn't forgiving. Until I made up my mind to forgive the individual(s), I wouldn't be free. Freedom has the ability to shape your own future by enabling personal growth, emotional release, and new opportunities. It encourages you to pursue your goals and dreams without the burden of negative emotions. With a freer mind, you can make decisions based on hope and positivity, not fear and anger. A freer mind is more adaptable and open to change. This flexibility allows you to handle life's ups and downs more effectively. Without mental constraints, you'll be able to think more creatively and you'll be able to explore new ideas and solutions.

By letting go of grudges and resentment, I became liberated from the emotional burdens that had hindered my personal growth and well-being. I was trapped in negative feelings and hurtful past experiences that were limiting my ability to move forward and make positive changes in my life. By choosing to forgive, I was able to free myself from constraints and was able to open the possibilities for a more peaceful and fulfilling future.

Personally, forgiveness completely shifted my perspective on life.

I refuse to allow my past hurts to hold me hostage.

Those past negative experiences turned into valuable life lessons, bringing a newfound sense of inner peace. Reflecting on it now, those internal negative voices grew louder, leading to daily negative reactions. I wonder what would have happened if forgiveness had been applied daily. Hmmm!

As I did a study, I came to the realization that unforgiveness brings on so many negative outcomes. A major negative outcome is your health. Unforgiveness can and will have a lifelong impact on our lives if we allow it. It can keep us stuck in negative emotions, like bitterness, resentment, and hostility, preventing us from experiencing joy, peace, and contentment. It can also create barriers to trusting one another. There are times when depression, anxiety, and heart problems, just to name a few, have become a part of the individual's life because they refuse to forgive. Then, there are some of us who are naturally more forgiving than others. I have considered myself, and still do, to be one of these individuals. I wasn't always this way, as you read in the previous chapters. I'll forgive and keep moving UNTIL I get to the point that I say, enough is enough. Some individuals will try to take advantage of your forgiveness if you let them. That's when you need to set boundaries. Boundaries, such as reflecting on what you need to do to feel safe and respected. Also, by sticking to your boundaries consistently, you create a stable foundation for your personal well-being and relationships. Wavering could send mixed signals and undermine the boundaries you already have set. Setting boundaries is a form of self-respect and self-care. There will be individuals who might challenge your boundaries, but stay firm and reiterate the importance of the boundaries for your own emotional health. By setting and maintaining healthy boundaries, you can practice forgiveness while also ensuring that your emotions and mental well-being are safeguarded.

Not by any means am I saying forgiveness is always easy, especially when the hurt is deep and when the other individual(s) think they haven't done anything wrong. Forgiveness is a process.

You read earlier in this chapter, the definition of forgiveness, but one thing I didn't elaborate on was having the desire for revenge. That's something to think about. If you have the desire, it's going to come to fruition. It's sad, but individuals seek revenge for so many reasons. Some seek revenge to restore a sense of fairness when they feel wronged or harmed. They also seek it because it provides a temporary emotional release, thinking it's helping to cope with feelings of anger, hurt, or betrayal. This is a big one! When individuals feel powerless or humiliated, seeking revenge can be a way to regain a sense of control and self-esteem. This happens more than we know. We have to recognize that getting revenge often causes more harm than good to yourself and others. Not letting go of the desire will allow you to continue a cycle of negativity and conflict. It pays to shift the focus from the wrong that was done to finding an outlet to help you heal. I have to check myself on a daily basis. I love what I read before…it stated,

Forgiveness doesn't change the past, but it can definitely change the future if you allow it.

Remember, forgiveness allows you to heal and move on. We heard this plenty of times that forgiveness is not for the other individual but it's for you. No matter if it's accepted or not, as long as you were sincere in asking for forgiveness.

Forgiveness doesn't always necessitate reconciliation. Forgiveness is a personal process that allows individuals to let go of anger and resentment, while reconciliation sometimes involves rebuilding a relationship and restoring trust, which may not always be possible or even desirable. It's about finding peace within yourself, even if it means maintaining a distance from certain people or situations.

Displaying forgiveness can be incredibly empowering and transformative, both for oneself and others involved. We sometimes can't control what happens to us, but we can control how we respond. What I'm referring to is that we can't control the actions of others, but we do have the power to choose our attitude and response to these situations. By focusing on our responses rather than the events themselves, we can maintain a sense of calmness. Let's look at it! When we face challenges and/or adversity, we have a choice to either be patient, optimistic, and proactive rather than giving in to despair or anger. What I like is this approach can lead to a better outcome and a more fulfilling life, as it helps us to navigate these challenges with a constructive and positive mindset. In my perspective, forgiveness gave me inner peace like no other. It made it easier to let go of past grievances and to foster a positive outlook on the individual(s). Why give the offender so much control and power? Forgiveness gives you the ability to take back your power from those who hurt you.

Forgiveness can be likened to a healed wound because it allows for closure and emotional healing, much like a wound, when healed, restores physical well-being and wholeness. I had to forgive myself for not knowing what I know now, and then came to the realization that I wasn't supposed to know; I was supposed to learn.

CHAPTER 4

"THE HEALING EFFECT"

The lotus flower is known for its large, fragrant flowers and distinctive round leaves. The lotus symbolizes purity, enlightenment, and rebirth. Even though it sits in muddy waters, the flower still blooms above the surface. When you look at the lotus flower, think about how you can rise above difficulties.

The healing process has begun. The *Healing Effect* refers to the process and outcomes of recovering from physical, emotional, and/or psychological wounds. Let's break it down! To heal physically is the process through which the body repairs itself from injury, illness, or any form of physical stress. Healing physically can also encompass adopting habits and treatments that support this healing process such as proper nutrition, rest, and physical therapy, just to name a few. Also, prioritize your self-care. Physically healing can help improve your mood and reduce stress. Also, I believe healing physically will allow you to engage in a new hobby or activity. This sometimes will help to discover a new passion and build a new sense of identity.

To heal emotionally and/or psychologically means to acknowledge. Recognizing and accepting the pain or distress you are experiencing is the first step towards healing. This means not suppressing or ignoring your feelings but allowing yourself to feel and understand them. Acknowledge that it's normal to experience sadness and anger but we should seek whomever or whatever we need to bounce back and not stay in that sadness and anger or whatever negative emotion it may be. Another way to heal emotionally and psychologically is to avoid negative coping mechanisms such as drugs alcohol, or even some type of unhealthy behavior. I was so grateful that I had the mind to turn to my God, and He gave me strength and direction on how to cope when the negative emotions tried to take over. Healing emotionally and psychologically is about restoring a sense of balance, well-being, and wholeness in your life.

The *Healing Effect* can often lead to a state of renewal, growth, and a better quality of life. The journey of healing and renewal can transform past pain into a foundation for a brighter and more empowered future.

The healing doesn't mean that the damage never existed, it means the damage will no longer control your life.

Part of the healing process is to acknowledge that past traumas and past pains can and will be a part of our history and more than likely cannot be erased. There are ways that can help individuals process and cope with them more effectively. However, healing involves reaching a point where these past experiences no longer will dominate our thoughts or dominate our emotions, and our actions. Instead of being controlled by past wounds, you find ways to move forward and regain control over your life. Healing is definitely about growth, acceptance, and finding strength despite what has happened.

Healing is a crucial part of life because the people around us don't deserve to bear the weight of our brokenness.

When we take the time to heal, we can interact with others in a more positive and constructive way. This prevents us from inadvertently placing the burden of our unresolved issues on those around us, which can strain relationships and create unnecessary conflict. Healing is not only just about fixing what's broken, it's about creating a life worth living. Creating a fulfilling life during the healing process is about integrating patience, self-compassion, self-care, and establishing a balanced schedule. The elements will allow you to find meaning and joy even in the midst of challenges.

While we're healing, we should undoubtedly celebrate your small victories and progress along the way. Small victories such as reclaiming some personal space and creating a new home environment that feels like your own. It might be just redecorating or just enjoying the peace of your space. Another small victory could be achieved by achieving independence like successfully managing tasks or responsibilities that you didn't handle before. This will boost your confidence and independence. But most of all, celebrate your own accomplishments, no matter how big or how small, as you progress toward your healing journey. Healing is a journey, not a destination, meaning that the process of healing is ongoing and continuous rather than something that has a clear endpoint. Keep in mind that each small victory is a sign of progress and growth. Eventually, these small victories will lead to a stronger sense of self and well-being.

Healing also means taking an honest look at the role you played in your own suffering. Acknowledging how our choices and reactions may have contributed to our own pain. It's about owning our part in the narrative to move forward in a healthier and more empowered way. When trying to heal from suffering it's important to recognize how certain behaviors and thought patterns might unintentionally contribute to prolonging the pain. Let me show you a few examples of prolonging your own suffering and/or self-sabotaging.

1. **Negative self-talk:** Continuously criticizing or blaming yourself can hinder healing.

- *Solution:* practice self-compassion and challenge negative thoughts with positive affirmations.

2. **Avoidance:** Avoiding painful emotions or situations can prevent healing.

- *Solution:* Face your feelings and seek to understand them. You can do this through prayer; therapy or even just journaling.

3. **Isolation:** Withdrawing from others can make the problem worse with feelings of loneliness and despair.

- *Solution:* Reach out to whatever or whoever will help you receive some laughter and peace. Get those endorphins going. These are just a few patterns I personally dealt with. After recognizing and addressing these patterns, it helped me to take an active role in my healing process that helped me foster a more compassionate and constructive path to recovery.

When you heal, the understanding of brokenness will come to fruition. True comprehension and insight into one's pain or difficulties often come after healing. Once an individual has moved through their process of recovery, they can look back and understand the reasons and lessons behind their suffering. What helped me to understand my brokenness was taking some time to acknowledge the parts of my life where I felt incomplete. After I acknowledged it, I had to accept it. Everybody experiences some form of brokenness, it's a natural part of being human. Being broken is often a temporary state, though it can feel enduring at the moment. Believe me! That's why the healing process is so important, especially to an individual who feels broken. The process can involve rebuilding one's sense of self learning to cope and move beyond the pain.

Healing often brings clarity and understanding. Healing also allows individuals to examine themselves, examining their thoughts, feelings, and behaviors. The self-reflection can uncover underlying issues and patterns that contribute to their brokenness. They learn more about themselves, their needs, and their desires which can lead to greater self-awareness and understanding. The process of healing can also help release suppressed emotions and alleviate stress and pain which can cloud your judgments and perspective. Healing also restores emotional equilibrium. This kind of healing helps to bring back a state of calm, reducing anxiety, stress, and emotional swings. It also involves processing and overcoming negative feelings. When your emotions are stable, it becomes easier to reflect on past experiences and understand them with a balanced perspective. However, letting go of these emotions can sometimes provide a clearer view of one's situation and experiences.

The self-reflection is crucial for personal growth and moving forward. By understanding and acknowledging your actions and choices, you can make meaningful changes and find a path to true healing. I had to and still am working on myself every day. One thing I love about healing is, it helps you become more aware of your personal needs, your boundaries, and strengths.

I previously spoke about self-care and the one thing I learned about becoming more aware of your personal needs is to be selfish. This may surprise you. But being selfish is not always a bad thing. As I mentioned earlier, being selfish in a positive way means prioritizing one's own needs, desires, and interests above others for your personal well-being. I perceive that when an individual starts to positively become selfish, they can't be manipulated so easily. There are some individuals who can't handle the fact that you decided to say "no". It needs to be about you at times. This healing process also taught me…

**That those who didn't know how to love me,
they taught me how to love myself.**

The healing process also connects your mind and body. I came to notice after doing a study, that the mind and body connection plays a significant role in the healing process. I believe it influences how the body responds to stress and illnesses. I also read and studied what is called the "placebo effect". The placebo effect demonstrates the power of the mind in physical healing. It can lead to symptom relief, improved health outcomes, and a better sense of well-being even though the treatment itself does not directly address the underlying condition. Listen up, when individuals 'believe' they are receiving effective treatment, their symptoms will begin to improve, even if the treatment has no therapeutic value or no value at all. It's what you believe. This effect emphasizes how the mind has an influence on the body's healing process. Very powerful!

Healing is a learning process. Healing from a divorce takes courage because it involves facing and processing a range of intense emotions. Through it, I have gained knowledge and insights about myself. Additionally, it helped me to understand the reasons behind my brokenness and to move forward.

Sometimes we can't heal because we blame others for our past and hurtful experiences. Blaming others is a common psychological defense mechanism. It allows individuals to deflect the pain and responsibility away from themselves, making it easier to cope with difficult emotions. Whether they're right or wrong. By blaming others, individuals seem to feel that their self-esteem and ego are protected. I also found out that some individuals grew up in environments where blaming others was a common way of dealing with problems and they have adapted this behavior as a coping mechanism. Blaming others for our past hurts can truly delay the healing process due to the fact that it'll keep us focused on the external sources of pain rather than addressing our internal responses and emotions. When this happens, I believe we relinquish control over our healing process, making it dependent on others' actions or apologies. Sometimes healing is learning how to forgive someone who never apologized. This can be challenging, but it can be done. We just have to acknowledge that we may never receive an apology, but by accepting this, your reality can help you move forward.

Whether it's through our insecurities or our thinking, we must come to the realization that our,

Hurtful experiences may be somebody else's fault but our healing is our responsibility.

I read a statement that said, try to heal without disturbing anyone. This statement right here was me all the way. Sometimes feeling like I couldn't talk to anyone, even though there were individuals, I could have poured my heart out to. But I just didn't want to put my situation on others. There were times I wasn't sure how I would be perceived because of my leadership status in the church, not that it would be any problem. Not only my status, but as an individual period. I also didn't want to impact those around me in a negative way. I definitely didn't want to overstep others and burden them with my issues. I was trying to stay private.

I started focusing on self-help techniques that didn't require extensive external support, even though I ended up seeking external support which became a value in my life. A few of the techniques were taking some time to be alone in some way shape or form. I would take a drive to a park and just sit and clear my thoughts. There were times when I didn't have the funds for gas so I started going to a window and gazing outside, no matter the weather, and started to be grateful. This helped me to change my mindset, as stated in chapter two. By applying these techniques, gratefulness became a habit, then it became me.

One of the things I really loved through my healing was, I started being aware of how I expressed my feelings and needs. It was my aim to communicate in a way that was considerate of others' emotional state. I started spending time alone to reflect on my personal growth activity without relying heavily on others for support. The main thing was I had to balance between attending to my very own needs and mental well-being before jumping to assist others. I did and still do try to stay away from any realms of toxicity. When you're in the healing process, you become aware of any toxicity that may come around you. You will start recognizing the signs of toxicity and understanding your emotional responses better. Red flags become more apparent. You'll become more adept at setting boundaries and maintaining them in order for you to not become a part of the toxicity.

I knew I was healing when I started responding rather than reacting.

This was powerful for me because responding rather than reacting brought on a shift toward mindfulness. I started to redefine what is normal and healthy. I began to appreciate the calm moments and the peace. The peace provided a stable foundation for my emotional health. Believe me, over time you will value the stability and the sense of security it brings. It showed growth in how I started handling situations and emotions. I responded to most situations calmly rather than reacting impulsively. I started to understand my emotions and triggers better. I didn't linger in down times. I would find myself bouncing back quicker with less distress. I felt more motivated to pursue my interests and passions. The inner peace and contentment were like no other. I started feeling joy in the little things like looking at the sun and listening to the birds in the morning. Just sitting in my car at a park looking at God's nature instead of looking at things negatively. When an individual is truly healing, the toxicity that tries to come about will change. Also, your perceptions will shift. Meaning, that initially there may be a focus on the pain and hurt, but over time, individuals often start to see past events as learning experiences rather than just sources of suffering. Additionally, the healing restores a sense of control and empowerment, making individuals feel more capable of handling future challenges. You will start to redefine what is normal and healthy.

My final stage of healing was when I felt the need to share my experience with others. Sharing my journey with others validated my feelings and experiences. It helps to know that others acknowledge and understand what I've been through.

The Lotus

The objective of **the lotus** is to follow the light

Growing towards it throughout the days and the nights

The lotus doesn't know the result...it just knows it feels right

Growing along its journey...what a beautiful life

Birthed in the dark...murky waters it never thinks to stray
away

The lotus just thinks... "nothing could be better than today..."

Still knowing the intention is not to stay...

Following the light...letting it lead the way...

Grounded and rooted in its murky environment...

The lotus is grateful for the time well spent...

Giving thanks as it serves **the lotus** as it was meant...

Moving on along the journey

Growing as it's supposed to be

The lotus gets a glimpse of the light

"Is this what's destined for me..."

Breaking through the surface...there's no words to explain...

Releasing the pain...only light to be gained...

Beginning to blossom one petal at a time...

Proceeding to unfold...the outcome is Divine...

The lotus is birthed...having risen into bliss

The night time exist...time to return unto the dark abyss

Only to be born again...until then

Rest for now my daughter...

We'll rise again when the sun hits the water.

Shu a.k.a Harrison

CHAPTER 5

WHEW CHILE!

"Whew, Chile," an expression often used to convey a sense of relief or being overwhelmed. It also is an expression to emphasize a strong emotional reaction to a situation.

The divorce was final, but there were mixed emotions, ranging from relief and excitement to uncertainty and sadness.

WHEW CHILE! Coming to the realization that someone can love you desperately with feelings and still not know how to love you correctly with their actions. This means that an individual might have deep and genuine feelings of love for someone, yet still lack the understanding, skills, and/or behavior needed to express that love in a way that is meaningful and fulfilling for the other individual(s). Essentially, loving someone emotionally is not always the same as showing love through supportive, considerate, and effective actions.

Acknowledging the intense emotions and difficulties I experienced during my divorce conveyed a sense of relief and emotional exhaustion. Not knowing what would be next in my life, how my children were going to be affected, and so much more. What happens when you make a decision that'll break your heart but will give you peace? Hmmm! ***WHEW CHILE!***

The emotional roller coaster really took a toll on me. I was exhausted from trying to be stronger than I felt. I was mentally, emotionally, and physically worn out from pretending to be more resilient or capable than I actually felt. The strain and fatigue were a result of suppressing true feelings. ***WHEW CHILE!*** I think about it this way, while the immediate aftermath might involve feelings of uncertainty, the long-term benefit of inner peace can lead to greater clarity, satisfaction, and authentic happiness.

After being married for twenty-eight years, not including the five years of courting, as mentioned previously, I was left in a state of shock and emotional numbness. At times, in unbelief, a short period of sadness, a long period of anger and resentment, as I stated earlier. A period of fear - fear of the unknown; a period of guilt and self-blame; a period of relief and liberation, still in this period. A period of confusion, having to adjust to a new way of life. I was no longer Mrs. I was back to being an older version of Denise Peterson. Also, a period of acceptance and I hope to discover new strengths and new opportunities. I was so mentally drained.

WHEW, CHILE!

I asked myself this over and over and over! If you stay somewhere where you don't feel complete, are you giving up on yourself? I believe that every situation is unique. Some might say yes, and others might say no. For me, the answer was yes. My future aspirations had changed. I wanted to feel free. I wanted to make choices that would prioritize my happiness, especially after years and years of putting others' happiness before my own. A great writer once said that happiness is a choice, not a result. Nobody on the earth can make you happy unless you decide to be happy.

Remember, your happiness will not come to you; it can only come from you.

I had to find myself! I had to constantly tell myself that *my peace matters. WHEW, CHILE!*

A singer once wrote, "You really don't know how strong you are until you have no other choice but to be strong." This is a very powerful statement. It shows the resilience and inner strength that people often discover in difficult times. When we encounter difficult or challenging situations, we often discover inner reserves of strength and determination that we were not aware of previously. Adversity can reveal hidden capabilities and resilience within us that we may not have recognized until we were put to the test. *WHEW, CHILE!*

You ask how you managed to become a better version of yourself. It was a long process for me because I was bitter for so long. I believe that the bitterness and emotional strain contributed to making the process feel even longer. I spoke to a trusted individual and prayed & prayed. As I mentioned in chapter two, I wrote that prayer is a weapon, but therapy is a strategy. Prayer was and still is the most powerful tool to use when coping with or combatting the challenges of going through a divorce. At the same time, therapy offered practical, professional human guidance for healing and personal growth. I used both! I would also take time for my self-care. Self-care isn't always getting my nails done or even going to the spa; at this time, my money couldn't go towards these activities, so my self-care was spending some alone time reading positive material and speaking affirmations to myself daily. Not only speaking but believing. ***WHEW, CHILE!***

Yes, negativity tried to come with any and every situation, but personally, I learned to combat that by living in the now, repeating, ***Living in the NOW***. I believe living in the now means fully engaging in the present moment without dwelling on the past or worrying about the future. It also involves being mindful and aware of your thoughts, feelings, and surroundings as they happen. Paying attention to the present moment helps you notice and appreciate the small joys and positives in your life while fostering a sense of gratitude that can counteract negativity. Also, by living in the now, you learn to accept the present moment as it is without resistance and it can help reduce the struggle against circumstances you cannot change, leading to greater peace and less negative thinking. Another reason you should live in the now is that when you're fully present, you are more likely to take positive actions that contribute to your well-being rather than reacting impulsively based on negative emotions. I feel by consistently living in the now, you create a mental space that is less susceptible to the impact of negative thoughts and emotions. It helped me to foster a deeper connection to life as it unfolded. Stopping to take some time to breathe and relax, and as a friend coach said, relax your shoulders; don't live so tense. Do you ever find yourself going about your daily lives but find yourself being tense for no reason at all? One time, I was driving and found myself holding on so tight to the steering wheel. Had to tell myself, relax! This happens more than we know. A lot of times, we go about our lives in tension, whether it be work pressures, financial concerns, or even health issues. We need to take some time to stop, breathe, relax, and begin being grateful for where we are NOW.

Living in the now gave me a sense of peace. Little by little, day by day.

Not searching for a new love in anything or any individual but searching on how to love myself.

WHEW, CHILE!

This journey has taught me to be resilient and strong by going through emotional challenges. It taught me self-awareness - how I gained a deeper understanding of my own needs, desires, and boundaries. This journey taught me about conflict resolution - learning to navigate disputes. When to talk and when to be quiet, still working on this one. It taught me independence - I had to discover new levels of self-sufficiency and independence. It taught me empathy - increasing my understanding of others. It taught me prioritization - I learned to prioritize what's most important to ME. This journey taught me growth - how to delve deeper into what I want my future to look like. It's taught me to embrace change. I had to understand that change is a part of life, good or bad, and embracing the opportunity helped me redefine myself and create a life that aligns with my true self. It also taught me to acknowledge my mistakes and how to take responsibility for my actions and behaviors. Most of all, this journey taught me how to LOVE ME. How do I build a relationship with myself first? ***WHEW, CHILE!***

Do YOU like YOU? Better yet, do YOU love YOU? What do you do if you're not sure of who you are? The greatest loss in life is when someone loses themselves. This was me at one time. What helped me besides reading my bible and other positive books, I had to stand back and start reflecting on my values and beliefs. I spent some time thinking about what matters most to me. I went back to journaling, as I did when I was younger. Journaling helped me to articulate my feelings. Writing down my thoughts and feelings helped me process my emotions in a safe place. I was able to organize my thoughts and gain clarity about what was going on in my life at that time. I still journal to this day. Finding your identity is a journey; it involves a 'continuous' process of self-discovery, growth, and adaptation over time, and it's okay to take your time and explore different aspects of yourself.

If there's something about yourself that you don't like, then please take the time to work on being a better version of YOU. Make sure you become proud of who YOU are. Building a relationship with yourself plays a very important step toward your own personal growth and fulfillment. Investing time and effort into understanding and nurturing yourself can lead to profound personal growth and a more fulfilling life.

Never give up on you.

I've learned that I didn't have to wait for everything to be perfect before I decided to enjoy my life. I remember being asked if I wanted to go on a girl's trip to St. Maarten. I immediately said yes, not knowing anybody but my cousin, whom I barely knew. We had just gotten reacquainted a few months earlier after not seeing each other for about 30 years, so this was a BIG step for me. Travel and adventure are some activities that are needed to assist people who are trying to find themselves after a divorce. Back to the trip - it was a phenomenal experience. Personally, it was a trip of healing. The individual, who spoke into our lives, to me, I saw as the "wellness coach." Every day was a different activity for us to strive toward our healing. My most favorable activity was done on the last day. She asked us to write down things we wanted to get rid of. We put them in a pail and burnt them. It was the most freeing and liberating activity. I came back home with a new outlook on things in my life. It feels good to live freely. Living freely feels like a breath of fresh air, where each day is filled with the excitement of new possibilities and the joy of making your own choices. Let me pause and say there are plenty of days when I'm not this excited. It's called life! We all go through challenging days - I won't say bad days, just challenging. You just have to find what's best for you to get you back to a liberating moment.

Okay, back to how I felt. I love the comfort of knowing that I'm in control of my own destiny, unbound by unnecessary constraints. By any means, I'm not saying you need to be divorced to feel this way. Not at all! There are plenty of ladies who are happily married and have this sense of freedom.

It feels good to walk in freedom over fear, freedom over anxiety, and especially freedom over the opinions of others.

These are a few more things that I had to apply to my life to help me stay free:

1. Reading daily! For me, it was and still is my bible and/or another motivational book.

2. Saying positive affirmations on a daily basis in the morning.

3. Letting go quickly of things or people that hurt us. (This was a tough one at times). Let me say this, there were times I didn't want to let go. Those are also the times when I open the door for bitterness to fester.

4. Learn how to react to things that have triggered me to speak or act in a negative way. This one right here - I'm still working on myself. ***WHEW CHILE!***

This book undoubtedly does not recommend getting a divorce. As I said, this was MY experience, and I pray that this book, in some way, would be a tool for better relationships with whomever it may be. Let us remember that we all need to work on being a better version of ourselves. Our personal growth is a continuous journey. It emphasizes the importance of self-improvement, reflecting on our behaviors, attitudes, and skills, and striving to become better in various aspects of our lives. This could involve learning new things, cultivating positive habits, improving relationships, and working on our mental and physical well-being. The idea is that everyone has the potential for growth and can make changes to lead a more fulfilling and meaningful life. How? By regularly evaluating your values, your goals, and your actions, you'll be able to understand what truly matters to you and align your life with those priorities.

Also, by defining what your goals are and making them clear and achievable, you will have a greater sense of purpose. Continuously seeking knowledge and striving to have new experiences. One thing that I feel is needed is to cultivate positive relationships with family, friends, and colleagues. Surround yourself with supportive and inspiring people. Additionally, you should focus on the positive aspects of your life, engage in acts of kindness, and contribute to your community in some way. Another way to lead a more fulfilling and meaningful life is to identify activities that'll bring YOU joy and make time for them.

JUST BE YOU in every aspect of your life. Understand YOUR values, your strengths, your weaknesses, and your passions. Stay connected to your true self. Be honest and genuine in your interactions with others. Avoid pretending to be someone you're not just to fit in or to please others. You have to know what is acceptable for you and communicate it clearly to others. Make decisions that are true to who you are, even if they are difficult; even though this may be challenging, you can do it. Trust in your abilities and beliefs. Don't be afraid to express your opinions and stand up for what you believe in. Most of all, I want to be the same person in different situations.

*My prayer is that we all heal from things
we haven't yet spoken about*

TO HAVE, TO HOLD, TO HEAL

Until……

A MESSAGE FROM THE AUTHOR

I believe in **YOU** and your abilities. You have what it takes to overcome any challenge. I wholeheartedly believe that God won't put any more on you than you can bear. As I mentioned in the earlier chapter, let us use our mistakes as lessons to learn. Remember, it's okay to have setbacks; they are part of the journey and can make you stronger. Dealing with setbacks can give you a deeper appreciation for the positive aspects of life and help you maintain a more balanced perspective. It all depends on your perception. **YOU** have a special inner power or resilience that is distinctively yours. This inner power is uniquely tailored to you, influenced by your history, personality, and the lessons you've learned along the way. It helps you to move forward with confidence and determination. Yes, situations happen in life to either discourage or encourage, but both negative and positive experiences contribute to who we become and how we navigate future challenges. It's all about how **YOU** respond. There's a quote I always tell my children - **YOU GOT THIS!** Just remember to be proud of yourself for how far you've come and never stop pushing to be the best you can be. God Bless!

ACKNOWLEDGMENT

Writing this memoir has been a journey of my reflection and my growth. I could not have completed it without the support and encouragement of so many wonderful people.

You know who you are.

First and foremost, I want to take this time to thank my family for their unwavering love and belief in me.

To those who listened, encouraged, and held space for me as I navigated the complexities of healing, thank you for your endless compassion and for reminding me of the light when I struggled to see it myself.

Lastly, to my readers, thank you for taking the time to journey with me through these pages. My hope is that these pages offer you comfort, understanding, and a reminder that you are not alone. Your support means the world to me.

With Much Gratitude,

Denise

ABOUT THE AUTHOR

Denise Peterson is a mother, speaker, CEO of her non-profit organization, and an advocate for women's empowerment. She is passionate and dedicated to sharing her journey of resilience, strength, and personal growth. She has always had a deep love for young ladies and women at large who face obstacles.

Her journey has not been without challenges. Through life challenges, she learned to navigate the complexities of life with grace and determination. Her experiences have shaped her into the resilient woman she is today, providing her with profound insights into overcoming adversity and finding inner peace.

In addition to her writing and being an advocate for women through her organization Women of Worth21, she uses her platform to inspire and empower others facing similar struggles.

This memoir is her heartfelt testament to the power of perseverance and the importance of staying true to oneself. Through her words, she hopes to connect with readers and provide a beacon of hope for those who are on their own journeys of self-discovery and healing.

Rediscover your strength and embrace the journey of healing with **To Have, To Hold, To Heal.**